BODMIN MOOR
AND AROUND

Terry Faull

First published in Great Britain in 2011

British Library Cataloguing-in-Publication Data
A CIP record for this title is available from the British Library

ISBN 978 0 85710 001 6

PiXZ Books
Halsgrove House, Ryelands Business Park,
Bagley Road, Wellington, Somerset TA21 9PZ
Tel: 01823 653777
Fax: 01823 216796
email: sales@halsgrove.com

An imprint of Halstar Ltd, part of the Halsgrove group of companies
Information on all Halsgrove titles is available at: www.halsgrove.com

Printed and bound in China by Toppan Leefung Printing Ltd

rney's church
e parish of
h Hill

Contents

How to use this book

Bodmin Moor can appear bleak and barren and so travellers who cross it along the central A30 main road might think that there is very little of interest or beauty to be found here. But they would be mistaken. The ten walks in this book are places around and about the Moor, chosen to show that the scenery is as beautiful as anywhere in the West Country and that the area is steeped in history.

The Moor has marshes, rock strewn slopes, craggy tors and great stretches of open rough grasslands. These are the haunt of lapwings and snipe, skylarks and ravens and where rare plants can be found. A thousand years before the birth of Christ, these uplands were extensively farmed; the remains of field walls, round houses and sacred stone circles built by the hardy families who lived here, can be found scattered across the landscape. A change in the climate caused most of these first settlements to be abandoned and by the Middle Ages, the high moor was used only for summer grazing. Villages and farms were now concentrated along the sheltered river valleys and people used a network of roads and tracks to trade, travel to church and move animals.

Originally known as Fowey Moor, until 1769 the only way across this wild country was a rough bridleway. This has now become the A30 dual carriageway

When weather and farming conditions improved, there was some return to the higher slopes. Later, in the eighteenth and nineteenth centuries, an increasing demand for tin, copper and other minerals led to extensive mining activities which have left their mark in many places across the Moor. Today Bodmin Moor is recognized for its unique landscape, as a refuge for nature and a place for quiet open air enjoyment.

The Walks

The walks in this book are suitable for those who enjoy a leisurely ramble and they provide a chance to discover the special scenery around and about the Moor. Most are along public footpaths and traffic free lanes and none is more than 5 miles long. They can all be tackled by walkers who do not regularly venture into wild countryside but who can climb stiles and do not mind sometimes getting a little muddy. Thanks to the Countryside and Rights of Way Act 2000, most of Bodmin Moor is now open access land; although some routes do take advantage of this right to roam, most of the walks are around the margins of the Moor across fields and through woodland. Some short sections are on local roadways where care may be needed.

Information is given about the terrain to be covered together with grid references to help you locate the starting point on Ordnance Survey Explorer map 109 which covers Bodmin Moor. There is a sketch map at the start of each walk and to add to the pleasure, snippets about the history and other features of interest are included.

Please follow the Countryside Code, respect those who live and work in the countryside, take care close to livestock, do no harm to the living and historic environment and above all, enjoy a time of quiet open air exercise!

Towards Brown Willy

Key to Symbols Used

Level of difficulty:

Easy ♥

Moderate ♥♥

More Challenging ♥♥♥

Map symbols:

Park & start

Tarred Road

Walk Footpath

River, stream or brook

Building

Church

Triangulation pillar or other landmark

WC

Refreshments

Pub

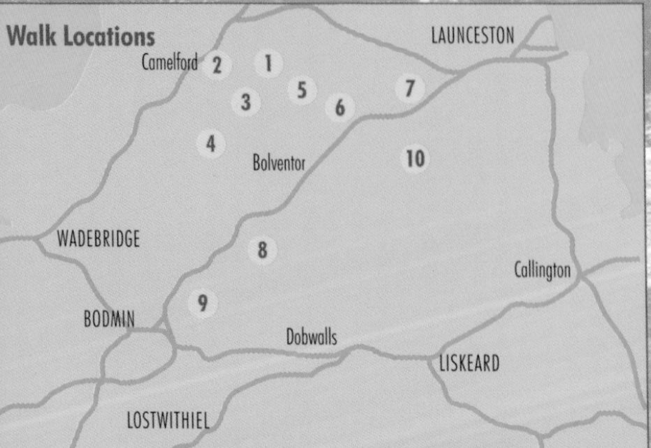

1 Roughtor

Open access moorland with Bronze Age remains, a memorial to a murder victim and spectacular hill-top views

Roughtor (pronounced 'rowter') is 1312 ft. (400m) high and from the summit, on a clear day, it is possible to see both the north and south coasts of Cornwall. Now the haunt of cattle, sheep, moorland ponies and wild creatures, it was once settled, and hut circles and ancient field boundaries remain as memorials to the first moorland dwellers.

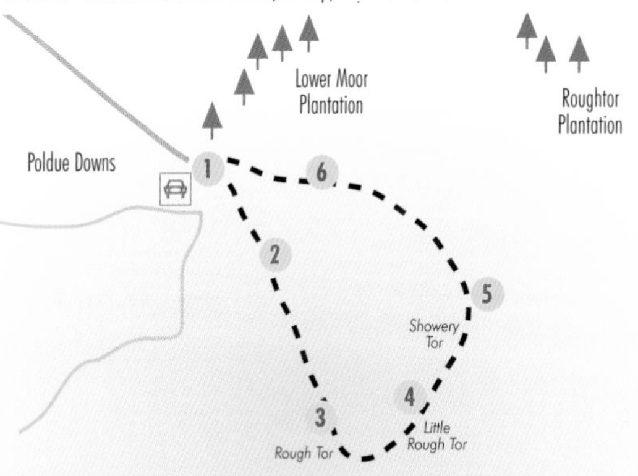

Level:

Length: 2 miles

Terrain: Moorland with some uneven slopes

Parking: Car Park at Roughtor

Start Ref.: SX 138819

The Charlotte Dymond memorial

1 From the car park a footpath leads down to a nineteenth century clapper bridge over a stream and out on to the open slopes of Roughtor. A few yards to the right of the bridge you will see a fence and beyond it a tall stone memorial to Charlotte Dymond, an 18 year old servant girl who was brutally murdered on this spot by her boyfriend in 1884.

The Moor at Roughtor

2 Make your way up the hill heading towards the main rocky summit. Here and there you will see the outlines of walls and hut circles which date from 2000-1500BC when a warmer and drier climate encouraged settlement and farming. These early house had low stone walls, a stamped earth floor and a thatched roof supported by wooden posts; the timbers and thatch have long disappeared but the remains of the circular walls can still be easily identified.

Hut circles

3 Closer to the summit, the slope become strewn with boulders known as 'clitter' or 'scree' produced by freezing and thawing during the last Ice Age. Pick your way carefully through this area and up to the Tor. A plaque attached to one of the boulders is a memorial to soldiers who served in the Second World War. Roughtor also has far older features of interest. A medieval chapel dedicated to St Michael together with a hut for a hermit, once stood here and we can only

Brown Willy gets its name from two Cornish words 'bronn' + 'gwennili' meaning 'hill of the swallows'.

Nineteenth century clapper bridge

imagine the rigours of a lonely life dedicated to getting close to God. From here Cornwall's highest point of Brown Willy (1375ft – 420 metres) does not seem far away and although it is possible to walk to it, our route turns along the hill to Roughtor's second summit.

4 Little Roughtor is some 10 metres lower than its sister hill but still affords some fine views across the Moor. On the slopes below, a line of low stone walls mark a defensive rampart which was built here during the Bronze Age; at about the same time, a number of ceremonial stone circles were built (the nearest one is at Stannon less than half a mile away) and these indicate that the Roughtor area was of particular spiritual importance.

A ford on the route

5 From Little Roughtor continue along the crest of the slope towards the next rocky outcrop at Showery Tor. The remarkable 'Cheesewring' formation here consists of molten magma from the earth's core which has cooled, crystallized and then contracted with horizontal and vertical joints. Weathered over millions of years to produce spectacular granite rock formations, similar ones are found in several places in Cornwall. Some known as Logan Stones, are so finely balanced that they can be rocked. Almost as remarkable is the massive man made cairn which surrounds Showery Tor. This 30 metre wide circle still stands one metre high and consists of a pile of stones which once covered one or more burial tombs. More than 400 cairns have been recorded on Bodmin Moor and together suggest that this was one huge sacred landscape.

6 From here it s a gradual descent back to the clapper bridge and car park. The vegetation is heavily grazed by the animals put out on to the Moor by farmers who have rights on the Common but here and there rare plants such as orchids and needle spike-rush can still be found. Birds such as linnets and stone chats take advantage of any grassy tussocks, while ravens and foxes can sometimes be spotted haunting the slopes in search of their next meal.

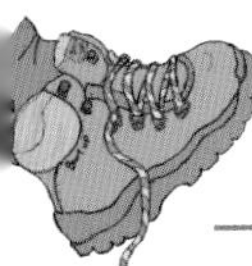

2 Camelford Riverwalk

An ancient river crossing, meadows and stone barns

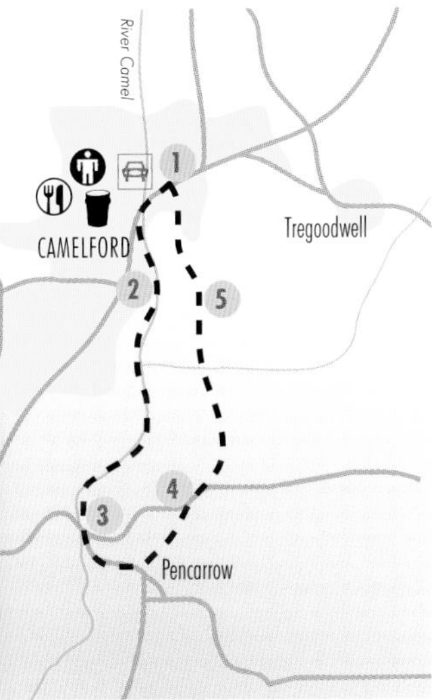

In times gone by Camelford was an important town on a crossing of the River Camel on the then main road into Cornwall. Its founding Charter was granted in 1259 and the town once elected two Members of Parliament. Today some fine buildings are a reminder of past importance and it remains a useful starting point to explore the Moor and the surrounding countryside.

Level:

Length: 2 miles

Terrain: Riverside paths, fields (one steep slope) and lanes

Parking: Free Car Park at Camelford

Start Ref.: SX 107838

The name Camelford refers to the river crossing here but it has nothing to do with hump-backed animals; the word comes from two Cornish words meaning 'crooked river'.

1 From the car park walk down into the town over the river. Note the rather fine town houses close to the bridge and the old Town Hall topped with a weathervane of a golden camel. It was built in 1806 as a market hall and was where a man once notoriously sold his wife for 2s 6d (it is believed that this

Old Town Hall

Camelford House

inspired Thomas Hardy, a regular visitor to nearby St Juliot, to include a similar incident in his novel *The Mayor of Casterbridge)*.

2 Continue uphill for a little way on the pavement opposite the Town Hall until you reach an archway between

River meadows

Footpath sign

the buildings with a sign reading 'To Advent Church and the river': turn down here and follow the river to the right. Footbridges take you across the river and then back to the original bank. The route follows the riverbank for about half a mile (past the sewerage farm!) and through meadows and woodland which are a haven for wildflowers and insects.

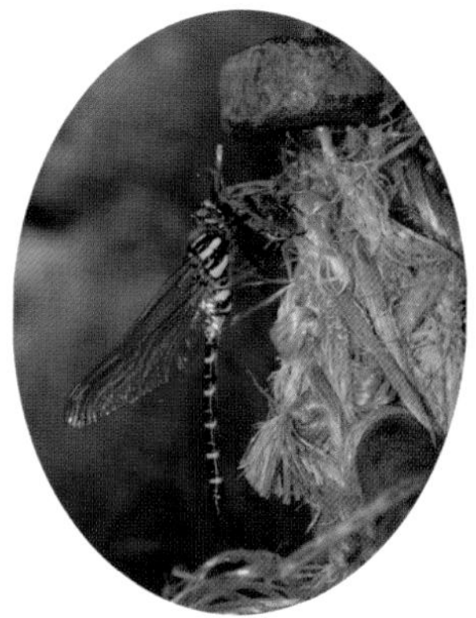

Above: Dragonfly resting

Below: Riverside path

3 Continue along the riverbank until you reach some steps up a hedge next to Fenteroon Bridge over the River Camel. Turn left over the bridge and then take the right hand fork in the road a short way to the hamlet of Pencarrow. This was once part of a medieval deer park and the place name means 'deer head' in Cornish. A footpath sign on the left will show you the way up some steps and you then cross two fields towards Treclago; just before reaching the road, note the rather fine stone wall and barn and the right.

Above: Fenteroon Bridge Below: Old stonework

4 Cross the road an turn into the lane on the left. There is another fine stone barn here, a reminder that Treclago is an ancient farm site with a history going back at least to the thirteenth century. Follow the lane, around a left hand fork and on into a large meadow where the path crosses towards an old metal gate then across a small field, over a wooden footbridge spanning a brook. From here bear slightly left up the slope, over a stile and head for the top left hand corner where another slate stile takes you on to a tarmacked lane.

5 Turn right down the lane past a number of residential properties. On the right you will see an old school; building; this is the site of the original Camelford College which was founded in 1679 by Sir James Smith and which functioned until 1962 as a local school (currently it houses offices for Cornwall Council).

Continue along the lane which becomes College Road and leads out on to the main road opposite the entrance to the car park.

Trecalgo Barn

The 80 square miles which make up Bodmin Moor include the warmest and wettest upland areas in Britain. The clean, warm rain has lead to its distinctive habitats and varied species of plants and insects.

The infant River Camel

Right: Fields towards Camelford

Dandelions and foxgloves adorn this handsome country stile

In 1784 Thomas Pitt, a cousin of the Prime Minister, was made Baron Camelford. The title died out in 1804 when the 2nd Baron was killed in a duel with a friend whom he believed had slighted a young lady.

3 Advent Circular

A Celtic site and its grim man, a devout community and a silver mine with royal connections.

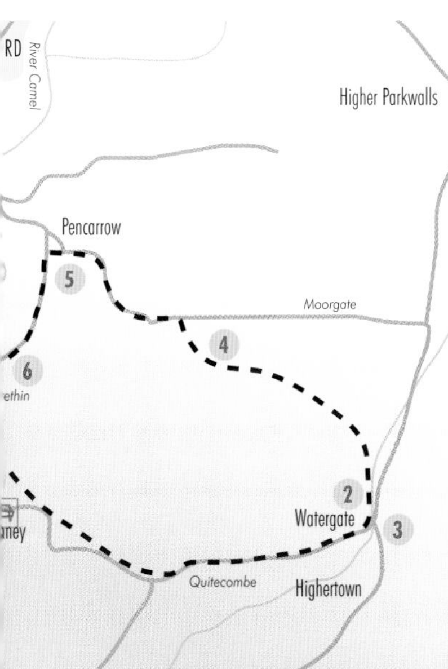

This moorland parish is dedicated to St Adwena but little is known about her except that in Cornwall she was the patron saint of sweethearts long before St Valentine. This walk provides some fine views of the Moor and its surrounding field systems.

Level: 

Length: 4 miles

Terrain: field walking and short road sections

Parking: Small car park at Advent church

Start Ref.: SX 104816

The distinctive white stones that can be seen in the hedgerows around this area are composed of quartz which is one of the main minerals found in the granite of Bodmin Moor

Advent church

1 As you enter the churchyard note that it is on a bank enclosed by a circular hedge which indicates that the site is an ancient Celtic foundation dating from the sixth century. The church itself is

Into the churchyard

The roof boss in the church porch at Advent

a mixture of ages and styles. It has a fine wagon roof, a Norman font and a particularly interesting roof boss in the porch of a man's grim face – perhaps reflecting a lack of favour from St Adwena! Cross the churchyard in front of the porch and out into a field through a small metal gate.

2 Aim slightly left diagonally across the field and over a stile, cross the middle of the next small field and with farm buildings to the right, cross three more stiles and fields and a stone stile on to the road. Turn left along the narrow roadway and follow this until you reach a junction at Watergate with its old granite bridge.

3 A short walk up the road to the right would lead you to Highertown and its tiny Methodist Chapel which was built in 1876 to hold 80 people and when many of the menfolk of the hamlet were lay preachers. Highertown overlooks the site of Stannon china clay works where pure white clay or kaolin was quarried for use in products like paper manufacture, pigments and plastics.

Highertown chapel

4 Our route continues at Watergate where you take the path alongside the river just before the bridge. After passing some old stone walls on the left, leave the river and after the next hedge, go diagonally across to the left corner of the field and into the next ahead and where you follow the left hand field boundaries until you reach a farm track. Walk along to the first stile on the right and cross into the field to reach the tall standing stone; called Long Stone, this dates from the Bronze Age (1500BC) and may mark a sacred site.

Granite bridge near Watergate

5 From the Long Stone, continue to the far left hand corner of the field and over the double stile on to the road. Turn left down the hill between the high hedges, past 'Gillings' and on to Pencarrow. Take the left hand fork through the hamlet and continue along the road for a short walk until you see the buildings at Trethin on your left.

Trethin meadow

6 A manor was recorded at Trethin in the fourteenth century when it was owned by the Black Prince. The current building dates from the sixteenth century and Trethin's royal connections were continued in the twentieth century when the estate was owned by Prince Chula of Siam (Thailand). In 1819 a silver lode was discovered here but the mine workings had to be abandoned because of flooding. Just past Trethin, a stile on the left will take you into a meadow with a pond (it supplied water for a wheel at the old mine). Cross the meadow to the trees and stream in the bottom left corner then over the large stone clapper bridge into the next field.

7 Walk up the hill where you will see the tower of Advent church ahead and cross back into the churchyard.

Advent church tower

4 St Breward

A moorland parish with a heart of granite, a wooded river valley and a holy well

The village of St Breward stands on one side of the deep valley of the River Camel and has developed from a number of hamlets which grew up around the church, farms and granite quarries. This walk provides breathtaking views of the countryside to the sea in the distance and then descends into the valley to find an ancient well once famed for curing diseases of the eyes.

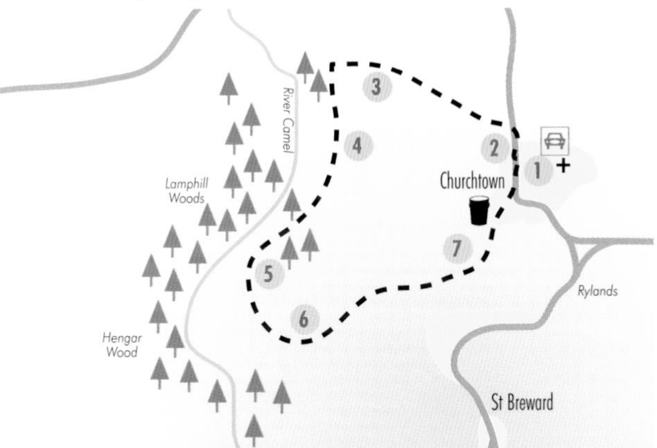

Level: ♥ ♥ ♥
Length: 2 miles
Terrain: Some steep and muddy tracks
Parking: Near the church
Start Ref.: SX 096774

1 There are a number of roadside places to park close to the church. St Breward or Bruered ('raven lord') who gives his name to the church and parish, was a Cornish or perhaps Breton saint of the sixth century. The present building has a number of Norman features including columns and a font but it is mostly of fifteenth century construction. The sundial over the porch and the carved heads by the tower door are especially interesting.

2 From the church turn right. The old building on the left of the road was the village stores from the late eighteenth century and in addition to groceries it sold boots and shoes, clothing and cattle feed. Set into its walls are a Victorian post box and also a rare yellow AA road sign (once common, most of these signs were taken down in the Second World War). Continue along the road for a short way then turn where a footpath sign directs you to the left.

Above: Tower door heads
Below: Sundial on church porch

AA road sign

Granite from the quarries around St Breward was used in many fine buildings including London's County Hall, Bodmin Gaol and Dartmouth Naval College.

e old village stores

Stile with curious pony

3 The footpath runs through some rough grassland and then straight ahead into a field and across to a granite stile which takes you into another area of land which is often grazed by moorland ponies as a way of keeping the vegetation in check. Make your way down across this area; a number of paths meet here but keep to the one which runs downhill and into the trees and then follow the stone hedge on the right.

4 Towards the bottom you will meet a track where you should turn left (ignore a another footpath way-mark which points to a path back up across the hill). Follow the track along the hill with its fine views down into the valley of the River Camel. The track soon

Above: Granite stone wall Below: Sunlight in a sunken lane

Old granite post

becomes a sunken lane through woodland and where there are some splendid examples of old granite gate posts and boulders which have been used along the route. Go through the gate at the end of the lane and out on to the road at Chapel.

5 The hamlet takes its name from the chapel of St James which stood here in the fifteenth century and which was one of the many places in North Cornwall which was dedicated to this patron of pilgrims. Turn left up the road; ignore the footpath sign which points to the right but instead continue for a few yards uphill and take the footpath signposted on the left.

6 Follow the path uphill until you reach the holy well. The small well-house is a fine structure and was once much visited by people seeking cures and good fortune from the healing spring.

Chapel Holy Well, St Breward

Unfortunately the water has been diverted away and now empties cold and unloved on to the road below. Leaving the well behind follow the steep track uphill until you reach a gate which leads you on to a lane next to a slate hung cottage on the left.

7 Turn up the track then shortly go through a field gate on the left and follow the waymark sign right and go across two fields and then over a granite stile on to a sunken lane. Turn left up the lane which takes you through a farmyard and out on to the road opposite the Old Inn. This hostelry has been the centre of village life for more than 200 years and a place where cattle and sheep from the Moor were bought and sold. From here return to the church and car.

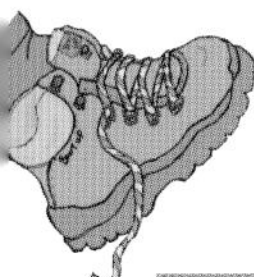

5 Bowithick

Carnivorous flowers, a link with wars ancient and modern, and the open Moor.

This walk, on the open Moor, begins at the picturesque hamlet of Bowithick on Penpont Water and where rich marshland is home to a variety of wildflowers and insects. Past old mineral workings and on to Buttern Hill to seek ancient stones and a view into the heart of High Moor and the source of the River Fowey.

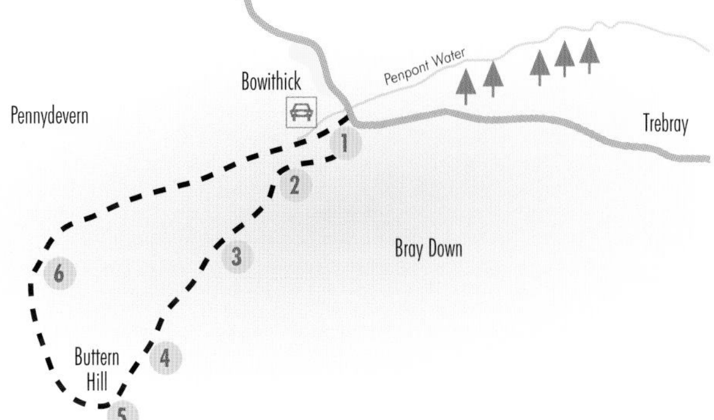

Level:

Length: 4 miles

Terrain: Open moorland walking with some damp places

Parking: roadside parking on the Moor at Bowithick

Start Ref.: SX 184827

An ancient stone cross stands at the road junction leading to the hamlet;. Bowithick means 'dwelling amongst the thicket'.

1 There is space to park on the grassland beside the the little stream at Bowithick and from here cross by the ford or bridge and on to the rough track which leads on to the Moor. Below the track you will see a number of stone bridges, earthworks and hollows where the stream has created a rich area of marsh-land on the site of old tin streaming works.

Three-arched bridge

2 The boggy patches here are a haven for wildflowers and insects and a special summer feature are the abundant sundew plants. Their fleshy, low growing leaves are covered with long red sticky hairs which are attractive to insects which become trapped and are then enveloped and digested by this native carnivorous plant. Continue along the track and up to the abandoned open mineral workings which are an obvious feature on the right of the slope of Buttern Hill ahead.

Sundew

Spaghnum moss and flowers

Bog cotton

Old mineral workings

Bray Down

3 These boulder strewn excavations are the remains of centuries of work to obtain the metal-rich ores of this part of the Moor. We know that ore from this area was used to make weapons more than 1500 years ago; a Bronze Age axe found in Sussex and a dagger from South Wales contain copper from the here. Simple 'streaming and washing' techniques were originally used to separate the heavier metals from lighter stones and excavations such as this are where the ore-bearing lodes were traced back into the hillside.

4 From the old mineral workings continue up the slope of Buttern Hill towards the summit. Near here a Halifax bomber on a training flight from Lincolnshire crashed in 1944; tragically the pilot died from injuries received in the crash. Look back and to the right towards the adjacent hill called Bray Down. There are old mining tunnels under Bray Down where minerals including uranium were once sought, and which were also considered as possible experimental sites during the nuclear bomb test ban negotiations in the 1960s.

5 Continue to the top of Buttern Hill where a careful search amongst the rocks along the summit will bring you to a stone cist (kist) or burial chamber. Stone lined graves like this one

Kist - burial chamber

have been found in several places on Bodmin Moor and almost certainly date from prehistoric times; the choice of such a remote spot and the effort needed to construct the chamber suggests that this was a high status burial, perhaps of a chief or spiritual leader.

Remains of an ancient cross

6 From here there are fine views across the Moor towards High Moor and Brown Willy beyond. The marshy area in the valley below is the source of the River Fowey and this may be one reason why the slopes of Buttern Hill were considered to be sacred by the early moorland dwellers. The route across the valley and on to Brown Willy should only be attempted by experienced and well equipped walkers, so our way back to the car is to swing left and back down the hill below Bray Down. Alternatively, swing right – and towards the hedgeline which marks the edge of the Moor and follow the infant Penpont Water back to the start near Bowithick.

Penpont Water

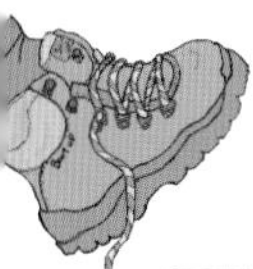

6 Altarnun

Cathedral of the Moor, an artisan sculptor, a cruel cure and a haunted house.

Starting beside the fifteenth century packhorse bridge and the historic church, this walk takes you through the pretty village, across fields and stone stiles and back by an ancient farm, and passes close to a special holy well and a haunted house.

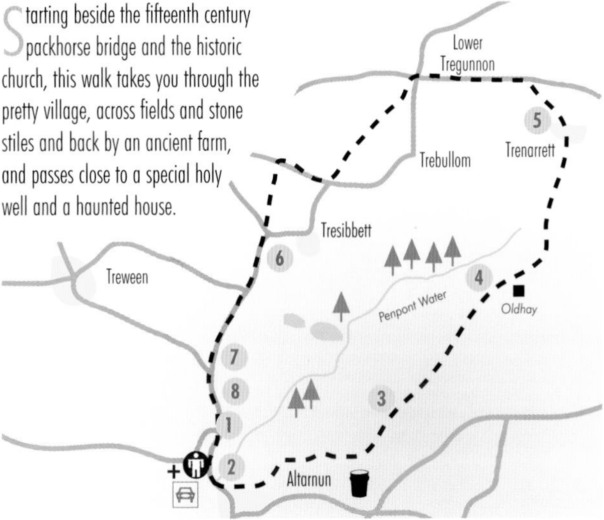

Lower Tregunnon
5
Trenarrett
Trebullom
Tresibbett
6
Treween
4
Oldhay
Penpont Water
7
8
3
1
2
Altarnun

Level:

Length: 5 miles

Terrain: Fields and lanes with road sections

Parking: Parking near the church

Start Ref.: SX 223813

John Wesley

Medieval packhorse bridge

1 The packhorse bridge which spans the fast-flowing Penpont Water, was one of the old routes to and from the Moor, and mounting steps remain from the time when horses brought travellers along the lanes to church. The current 'church' building mostly dates from the same period as the bridge but is built on the site of a much earlier structure. Its origins possibly go back as far back to the time of the Celtic saints such as Nonna, who was the mother of St David of Wales, and who gave her name to this place. The church of St Nonna is often called the Cathedral of the Moor and its tall tower, fine carved bench ends, wagon roof and rood screen are certainly the most splendid in the whole area.

Above: Cathedral of the Moor
Below: Old Methodist Chapel

2 Cross over the bridge into the village and make your way up past the attractive cottages with a stream at their front doors to the old Methodist Chapel near the corner. Above the door is a carving of John Wesley who was a regular visitor to this area. The carving was made by Neville Burnard, son of a local stone-mason, and who later became a celebrated sculptor. Exhibitions of his work were shown at the Royal Academy, he was introduced to Queen Victoria and had work commissioned by many prominent Victorians. After the tragic death of one of his daughters, he turned to drink and ended his days as a pauper in the Redruth workhouse.

3 Just below the old Chapel, take the signposted footpath between

the cottages, one of which has a millstone at the threshold of the porch. Go through the gate and stile and across the middle of the field to the stile in the far hedge. Bear diagonally left across the next field to a stile in the left hand corner and then straight ahead by the left hand hedge to the farm buildings. Pass over the stile to the lane in front of these buildings to the cluster of converted barns at Tresmaine. Pass through Tresmaine along the track and at a T-junction turn right for a few yards to the gate which leads into the field. Follow the waymark signs across the centre to the next stone ladder stile and then follow the left hand hedge for two more fields. After another stile go across middle of the field to the left hand corner where a waymark post directs you left to

Above: Millstone at the threshold, Oldhay
Below: Barns at Oldhay

and across to a narrow field-gate. Keep to the left hand hedges to reach Oldhay. The footpath here has been diverted around the back of the buildings.

4 Oldhay farmhouse is a listed seventeenth century building and the barns associated with it suggest that this was once an important farm. The old

pulley at one end of the barn shows that the machinery here was originally belt driven and as you walk down hill from here you will pass some granite blocks which may once of held a driving shaft powered from a waterwheel below. At the bottom of the hill you will reach some stone steps set into the hedge ahead; before you climb these look out for the deep waterwheel pit just to the left of the path.

5 After the stone steps cross the field to the foot bridge and then follow the waymarked path up towards Trenarrett. Go in to the fenced off path on the right of the gate and join the track; turn left at the junction by Lower Trenarrett and shortly over a stile which leads into several small enclosures. At a barbed wire fence turn left and then over an old stone stile into the next field where you bear right and across to the top left hand corner and a stile on to a road. Turn left along the road for a short walk to the crossroads at Lower Tregunnon.

6 Here you take the left fork but at once go over a stile on the right and into a field. The route now goes across five fields to rejoin the road further along. After climbing down the steep stile on to the road, turn sharp right up an unmade 'green lane' and continue until you reach the point where there are stiles on either side of the track. Take the left hand stile into a young woodland and then into the field and across the left hand corner and stone stile which takes you back on to the road by a junction. Here you should turn right down hill along the road. Ignore the first turning on the right and continue to the next junction near some houses where you turn left downhill towards Altarnun.

7 As you walk downhill look out for a place where the road widens on the left and with an entrance with ornate field and a pedestrian gates. A diversion off the road here will take you to the site of St Nonna's Holy Well. Today all that remains here is a rather overgrown pool

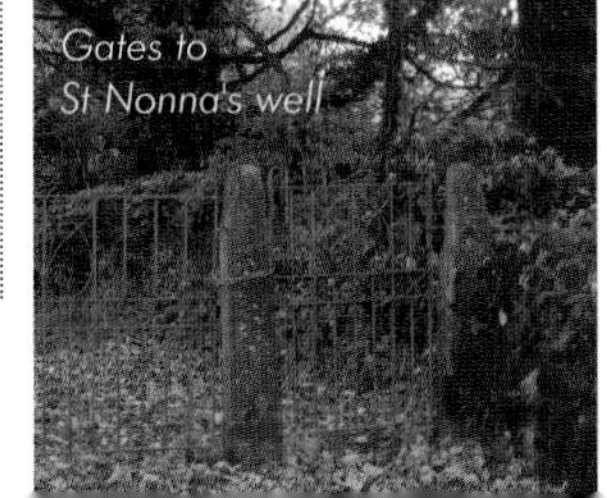
Gates to St Nonna's well

behind a low wall but once this was the place where people suffering from insanity were bound and repeatedly thrown backwards into the water in the hope of a cure. Known as a 'bowsening' the practice was described in the sixteenth century but thankfully fell into disuse and the spot was allowed to fall into ruin. Today the holy well of St Nonna at Altarnun is a peaceful place of escape from some of the madness of the modern world.

8 Continue downhill back to the church. The splendid house on the right just before you reach the starting point of this walk was once the Vicarage and local legends tell how it is haunted by the ghosts of a Victorian vicar and the servant girl with whom he had an affair. She later drowned herself in the river nearby; let us hope these two poor souls, like the unfortunates who were cast into the bowsening pool, have at last found their peace in the beauty and stillness here.

The haunted house?

7 Polyphant and Trewen

A holy way, an ancient source of stone, a medieval chapel of ease and a village green.

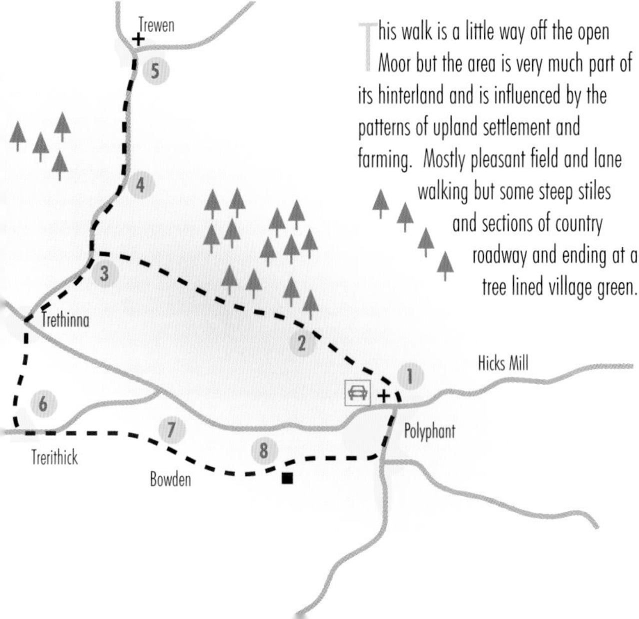

Trewen
5
4
3
Trethinna
2
1
Hicks Mill
Polyphant
6
7
8
Trerithick
Bowden

This walk is a little way off the open Moor but the area is very much part of its hinterland and is influenced by the patterns of upland settlement and farming. Mostly pleasant field and lane walking but some steep stiles and sections of country roadway and ending at a tree lined village green.

Level:

Length: 3 miles

Terrain: field walking and short road sections

Parking: Car park at rear of the chapel

Start Ref.: SX 263822

In the Cornish language Polyphant means 'pit of the toads'.

1 One of Cornwall's ancient crosses, known as Holyway Cross, stands next to the main A30 road at the turning into Polyphant. The cross probably dates from the fourteenth century when it was erected to mark the rough track which at that time was the only route across the middle of Bodmin Moor. At Polyphant the Methodist Chapel is also used as a community centre and from the car park at the back of the building, turn left along the lane.

2 As you walk up the lane you will pass a number of fenced off gateways on the right of the track. These are entrances to old quarry workings which are spread along the hillside and which are the source of Polyphant stone.

Above: Polyphant Chapel Below: Polyphant quarry

A kind of soapstone, it can be readily carved when first quarried and has been much used since at least the time of the Normans; pillars and fonts made of Polyphant stone are found in many church buildings across Moor and elsewhere in Cornwall and Devon.

3 Continue along the lane, past a house and woodland on the right until you come to a field gate. Go through this and then cross the centre of the field to the hedge opposite; this is the boundary between the parishes of Lewannick and Trewen and may date from the Anglo-Saxon period. You will find a series of stone steps which form a stile to take you into the next meadow where you should follow the lower long hedge until you

Above: Stone steps up the hedge
Below: Trewen mill

reach the stile and gate on to a narrow country road. Turn right here and follow the road downhill (if you wish to shorten this walk turn left uphill to reach point 7).

4 After a short walk downhill along the narrow road you will reach a pretty little bridge over the River Inney. Just over the bridge is Trewen Mill; now an attractive home, it was the site of a

tragedy in the nineteenth century when the dress of wife of the miller got entangled in the shaft of the waterwheel and she was drawn in to her death. Walk on past the mill and up the road until you reach the hamlet of Trewen and its church.

5 Dedicated to St Michael and All Angels, this little church has a fascinating history. Standing within a circular enclosure which is slightly higher than the surrounding land and with a holy well in the lane to the north, this has all the hallmarks of a Celtic Christian foundation dating from the fifth century. The building we now see dates mostly from the fifteenth century and was originally a chapel of ease (a building used for worship by local people who could not easily travel regularly to the parish church) founded by Launceston Priory. Trewen church saw bloodshed in the fifteenth century during a quarrel between two local wives but today is a haven for quiet peace and prayer.

St Michael and All Angels Trewen

6 Leave Trewen and return downhill, past the Mill and back to the point where the walk left the field at Point 3. Carry on up the road to the hamlet of Trethina where a number of the fine old farm buildings have been converted into accommodation. At the junction ahead, turn left and walk a short way until you see a footpath sign pointing to the right. Here you will see some a stile between two rather fine stone pillars and this will take you into a field; keep to the right hand hedge which will lead you on to a

Stile with pillars

track and through a gateway into the farm complex at Trerithick. Many of the farm buildings around the listed manor house have similar protection and here and there in the walls there are old windows and doorways which hint at the once high status of Trerithick. Walk around the outside of the barns and past the back of the manor house (the magnificent tulip tree in the garden is probably one of the first planted in Britain) and note the ornate windows and chimneys before going out on to the road.

7 Turn left and along the road for a very short walk to the footpath sign pointing right up some steps in the hedge. Walk across the middle of the large field towards a line of some old trees growing on the remains of an ancient hedge boundary and then straight across to the far hedge where a stile and stone steps will take you into the next field. Head towards the left hand corner of the buildings of Bowden Farm which you can see ahead of you and when you reach them, go out on to the farm lane. Turn right past the buildings and farmhouse. When you reach the modern part of the farmyard look out for the path which is on the left.

Old barn window

Trerithick

Parish boundary hedge

8 Take this path and keep to the left hand hedge across a field until you reach a gate leading into a narrow green lane. Follow this until you see the entrance to the complex of Bowden Derra on the right. This was originally the centre of a fine country estate but today the house and surrounding buildings are being put to good use as a residential home. Keep straight ahead and out down the drive and you will eventually reach a short section of footpath on the left which will take you between some cottages and out on to the village green at Polyphant.

9 Village greens such as this are not very common in Cornwall and it is a credit to the local community that it is kept in good condition. Cross towards the telephone box and just to the left you will see a public footpath sign which takes you past some cottages and a short walk to the road and the chapel where our walk began.

Village green

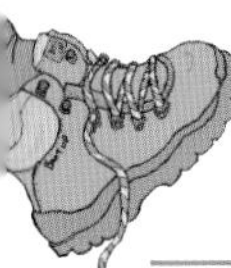

8 Warleggan

A gateway to Narnia, turbulent priests and a Gothic revival house.

Sometimes described as the most remote village in Cornwall, tiny Warleggan can still only be reached along narrow lanes and it is no surprise to see on its village sign a boast that it is twinned with Narnia! In the past it has been the home of some eccentrics and retains a special atmosphere of its own. This is a short walk along rutted tracks and steep slopes but very worth the effort.

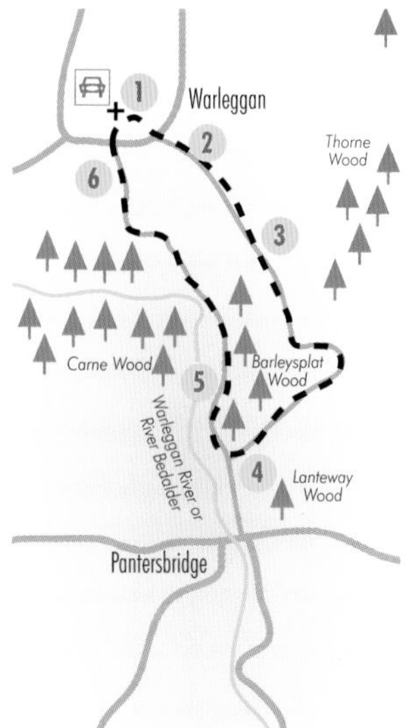

Level: ♥♥♥

Length: 1.5 miles

Terrain: Rough tracks

Parking: Small car park by the church

Start Ref.: SX156691

In the north wall of Warleggan church is a blocked up fourteenth century doorway and according to legend, doors in this position were Devil's Doors where the Devil was driven out during baptism.

1 St Bartholomew's sits in a circular churchyard, this is known as a llan and a sure indication that the site is of Celtic origins. The seventh century wheel-headed stone cross near the entrance was moved to here in the nineteenth century and may once have marked a pilgrim path to Warleggan across the moors. The church has been remodeled on several occasions including in 1818, after it was struck by lightning. A vicar in the fourteenth century robbed the church of its goods then tried to burn down the parsonage; a more recent incumbent in the 1950s quarrelled with his parishioners after which it is said that he preached only to a church full of cardboard cut-outs of worshippers!

Above: Seventh century cross

Left: 'Narnia' village sign

2 On one side of the parking area by the church you will see an old painted doorway which was once used by the eccentric twentieth century priest to reach his rectory. Through the field gate on the other side, you will be able to see a small stone building which is known locally as 'The Band Room' and which probable began life in the eighteenth century as a parish meeting place – it is undergoing a major restoration programme which should restore it to community use. Take the narrow path just below this field which will bring you on to the road next to a row of attractive cottages with a village pump. Cross over the road and on the left undo the chain to go through the metal gate which leads on to a track.

Door to the old rectory

3 Follow this narrow path downhill between high hedges. Underfoot it becomes very rough and stony but nevertheless there are sometimes tyre marks which show that some adventurous drivers have come this way, no doubt taking advantage of the uncertain status of the lane with its permitted public access.

Circular llan churchyard

Cottages and village pump

4 Continue down the lane and follow it around to the right just before it reaches the stream at the bottom. The way now skirts Barleysplat Wood (the name possibly comes from the Cornish 'bedewen' meaning birch tree, although a 'splat' also refers to a small field in the Cornish language) and then out on to a surfaced lane by an attractive bridge over the River Bedalder.

Warleggan gets its name from a word in Cornish language (Gorlegan) meaning 'high place'. The highest point in the parish is Carbarrow Tor, just north of the church, standing at 912 feet.

5 Turn right here. After a short walk along this lane you will come to Barleysplat Farm on the left. You will wish to respect the privacy of the occupants but, as you pass-by, notice the extraordinary building which abuts the lane. Once just a cob and stone cottage, it has been completely transformed in the Gothic revival style using reclaimed materials including from Victorian churches. It was the home of members of the Brotherhood of Ruralists, a group of twentieth century artists, crafts-people and poets and has featured in several magazines and television programmes.

6 Continue along the lane uphill until you reach the road just opposite the entrance way to the church.

Gothic revival wall

9 Cardinham

An ancient stronghold, early women's rights, stone crosses and woodland walks.

Soon after the Norman conquest of Cornwall , a motte and bailey castle was built here as the home of Turold, an important knight (he may be the hunch-back shown in the Bayeux Tapestry). His family changed their name to Cardinham to reflect the two ancient Cornish words of their new home – 'ker' meaning fort and 'dinan' also meaning fortress. In the Middle Ages women here were exceptionally allowed to keep their lands and property if their husband died. This walk is a pleasant stroll from the church across fields and into woodland with links to a network of Forestry Commission walking trails.

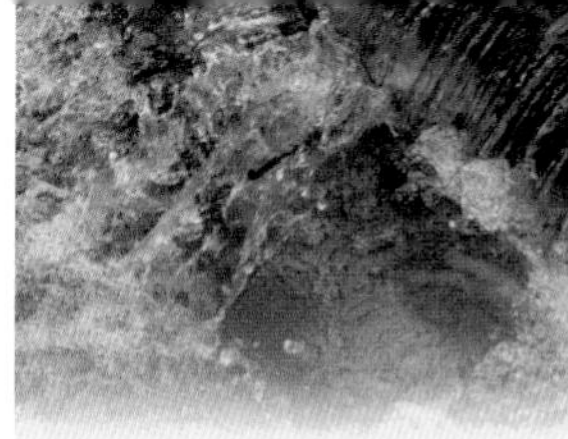

Level:

Length: 2 miles

Terrain: Field and woodland walking

Parking: By the parish hall opposite the church

Start Ref.: SX124686

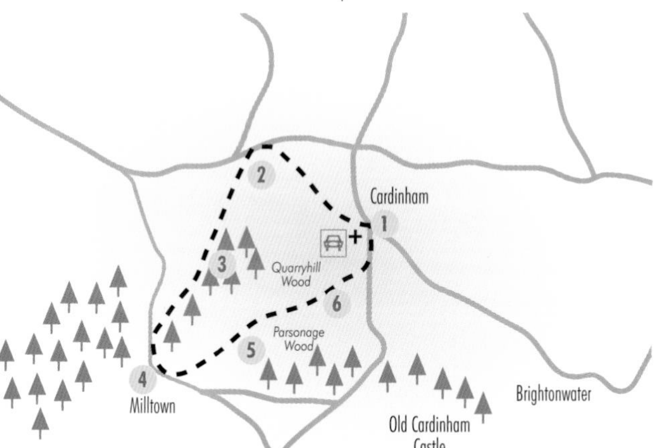

1 Striking features at Cardinham church are two stone crosses in the churchyard; the oldest one, by the porch dates from 800AD while the base of the near the main gate may be a little more recent. Both are witness to the faith of St Muebred, a fifth century hermit who

Cardinham church

There are 4 ancient inscribed stone crosses in the parish of Cardinham which suggests this area was a spiritual as well as a military centre for the Moor from early times.

tradition says was brought here for burial after being beheaded in Rome. The church itself is worthy of attention including a medieval brass memorial to Thomas Awmarle who, although a rector, is shown wearing a sword to mark that he was of noble birth. Leave the churchyard through the gate close to the porch and turn right along the track to a field gate.

2 From here walk ahead and down the sloping field across to the stepping stones and stile in the far hedge. Turn left over the road bridge across the

Ancient stone cross

Stepping stones and stile

stream and then left through a field gate. With the stream on your left, walk across this field and up the hedge and stile into the woodland beyond.

3 Follow the well worn track and lane through the woodland. This area is a haven for wildflowers and birds and if you are very lucky (and quiet) you may see a deer or fox. Continue until ahead you see a forestry road and marker post; this roadway is part of a complex of routes through Cardinham Woods which have

Hedge and stile

been developed as walking and cycling trails. However, our way follows the sunken lane which turns left here.

4 Shortly after turning down hill, the track reaches the stream, called Cardinham Water, which you can cross by the ford or over the striking clapper bridge of great granite slabs. Ahead is Langsmill and Milltown. The corn mill here is the reason for the network of paths and roadways which converge at this spot. After crossing Cardinham Water go past the cottage on the right then shortly after, take the footpath on the left of the road.

5 Walk along the path and cross the little stream and up into the field ahead. Cross this meadow and then into the next field where you should aim slightly to the right uphill until you reach the stone hedge, follow this to the right. As you go, admire the ancient trees here and note how the landscape is becoming more formal and park like.

6 By following the stone hedge on the left you will soon reach a gate into another field where the line of an old track can be seen running across the centre on the enclosure and towards a striking house on the far side. The walk across this field provides some fine views towards the church and also of the site of Cardinham House and gardens on the left. Pass in front of the house ahead of you and join the road where you turn left and will soon reach the starting place.

Right: The ancient clapper bridge

Primroses in the wood

Cardinham church from the path

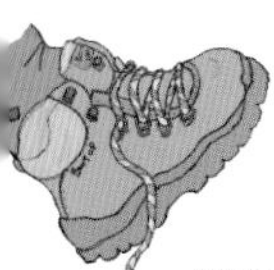

10 North Hill

A mysterious saint, a Domesday manor and a test of initiative to reach a Tor.

From the attractive village this circular walk passes through fields and woodland, over the River Lynher and eventually out on to the open Moor and then back past ancient enclosures in a landscape. This takes the walker through lands once gifted to Glastonbury Abbey by an Anglo-Saxon king.

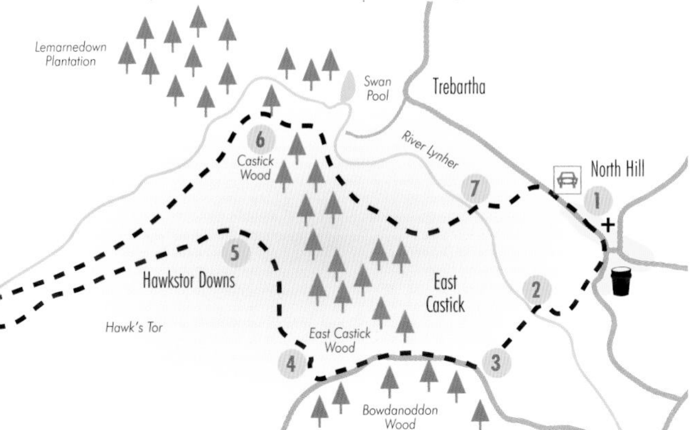

Level: ♥♥♥

Length: 4 miles

Terrain: Rough tracks and moorland

Parking: Car park by the village hall

Start Ref.: SX273766

Memorial statue

1 The village hall at North Hill has spaces for public parking. From here the walk commences across the bottom of the playing field towards the church and out through the gap and then into the churchyard. The patron of the church is the unknown Saint Turney or Torney, a name not recorded here before the eighteenth century but is probably the same holy man who has been remembered elsewhere in Cornwall since the thirteenth century as St Erney. This is a magnificent granite church with an imposing porch with a sundial and vaulting in the roof. Inside there is much to admire including a family memorial with almost life size statues of a man and his wife at prayer.

St Turney's church

Sundial on church porch

2 From the church go back on to the road and take the right hand turn down past the Methodist Chapel (dating from 1810) and short way to the public footpath sign on the right. Follow

the path through a kissing gate and down across the centre of a field to the stile which take you into the woods. Down some steps, straight across a track and then down some more steps, across a

New footbridge

footbridge and then to the River Lynher which can be crossed by a splendid wooden footbridge which was put in place in 2010. St Turney's holy well is tucked into the bank below the track some 75 yards downstream from here but unfortunately it is not reached by the public footpath.

3 After crossing the river, follow the path right and up through the woods. This is part of the Trebartha estate which has been here since the manor was listed in the Domesday Book in 1086 and before then was part of the land known as 'Linig' (island land) which was owned by Glastonbury Abbey having been given to it in 710 as a gift from King Ine after the Anglo-Saxon occupation of this part of Cornwall. The route takes you up to a field

Entrance to the holy well

where stile in the right hand corner leads on to a farm track. Cross straight over and into a narrow strip of woodland and along a path to another field where the right hand hedge will lead you through a kissing gate on to a tarmacked road.

Hawk's Tor

4 Turn right up the rather steep road and as you walk along, notice the moss and fern covered hedge bank on the left. After approx. ½ a mile and towards the brow of the hill, a footpath and bridleway sign on the right will point you into some rough ground. You are now in the 'foothills' of Hawk's Tor and the open Moor. The track bends slightly to the right and after a short way you will find a number of pathways and this is where you can exercise some initiative! Hawk's Tor is open access land and you are free to make your a way up the slope to the craggy summit where there are splendid views across to Twelve Men's Moor and Kilmar Tor. Do stop to admire the trees hung with grey/green lichens, an indication of the clean wet air of the Moor. If you go to the top you can rejoin the route on the other side by finding your way down the boulder strewn slope.

5 Alternatively, keep to the track ahead, over a stone bridge across a little stream and out across two small rock strewn fields. In the top hedge you will find a small gate which leads out on to the Moor. The rough track ahead follows the contour around the hillside of the Tor. The way lies through rhododendrons and you will soon see the summit of Hawk's Tor above on the left hand-side. Continue ahead keeping a stone wall on the right until the point where the wall

North Hill from Hawk's Tor

veers right; follow this wall until you almost reach the stream when you should turn right into the marshy ground and on into a field. Cross the field to the top right hand corner where it joins the open Moor and then across the centre of the next field towards the woodland.

6 A gate will take you on to a trackway which goes through the Castick Woods alongside a number of stone walls which are said to have been built by French prisoners of war captured during the Napoleonic War. Follow the track until you reach a gate on to a concrete farm road. Turn right up this road until you reach Castick Farm where you pass through the farmyard, bear slightly right and over a stile and then across to

Castick Farm

fields towards the corner of a wood. After a gate, follow the hedge left and into the next field where on the far side and straight ahead you will find a footbridge over the Lynher.

7 From the footbridge go slightly right pass an oak tree in the middle of the field and then up the steep wooded bank ahead to a stile into the final field where the way straight across will bring you to the road. Turn right and you will soon be back a the Village Hall.

View from the final footbridge